WELCOME

I had forgotten how amazing life and everything in it is; the people, the creatures, the weather, the scenes, the experiences. However, this world came about, I applaud the creativity and beauty that everything in it holds. There's no fucking way, if we exist in this incredible world, that we are meant to live unhappy, bothered and unfulfilled. We got this shit all wrong, and if life seems to be one struggle cycle after another, or if you've got it all but still feel anxious, empty, unhappy or lost, read this book because I was able to figure something out and I believe I can help others do the same. This isn't a "life improvement" type of book. You're not just going to read this book and all of a sudden, your world will change. What I write in this book is my exact experience and knowledge of shifting into a much-heightened awareness. This isn't hard people, you have the knowledge inside of yourself and if you follow what I have done, you will shift yourself. This is a change your inside world type of journey while experiencing your outside world change with it. Without having to make much effort, it will just start happening....all you need is an open, clear mind. But in order to attain an open and clear mind you must understand that you do have thoughts that are taking up most of the space and those old thoughts and ideas of life are gonna need to be put aside. We all think way too much and we think absolutely irrelevant shit that usually just upsets us. If everyone walked around speaking their thoughts, we would all look wacko.

Your ideas of the outside world are going to completely change once you clear out your thoughts. Life is experienced from the inside. Everything you hear, touch, taste, smell, see, and experience is all happening inside of ourselves; our emotions and thoughts are also happening inside of ourselves. And I believe that whatever you feel and think on the inside affects how and what you experience on the outside. It's all in how we perceive our individual life; our perceptions of life create our experiences, and with research and practice, I have transformed my perception. By observing my own behaviour, thoughts and emotions, I was able to come up with practices that have shifted me into a different existence. I'm experiencing a completely different life but nothing really outside of myself has actually changed. My mind cannot find words to describe it, but the closest I can get to is dreamy, sometimes trippy in the thrilling kind of way, peaceful for sure, joyful, light hearted; I'm experiencing my outer world morph and align with how I think and feel inside and it's just incredible.

I wrote this book for those who are seeking some kind of realization and enlightenment and aren't quite sure what to do. Maybe you've been trying but high expectations and goal setting began to discourage you or maybe you just don't know where to start. You have it within yourself to completely upgrade your view of life, the realizations are inside you, and this book will help you recognize them for yourself. I went from having little control over my emotions, over my thoughts and over much of my actions, to vanquishing all of the bullshit thinking, no longer overreacting, unbothered by almost everything that used to bother me and feeling centered and connected; feels like freedom.

Many of us have layers of programmed information stored in our brain that is blocking a clear view of life. These layers were imposed on us from day one; we have been taught by outside influences how life works, when in truth they themselves don't really have much of a clue on how this world and life works. I've succeeded at de-programming my mind of bogus thoughts and ideas of life, and I see more than I could have ever imagined. I did this by practicing different behavioural changes; anytime I was faced with conflict, either within myself or with the outer world, I broke down each situation and worked at changing my whole my perspective on it. I shifted from the practices and the world will never be the same for me.

I know that some may be hesitant in getting into their own minds for reconditioning, but I can tell you first hand that there is no loss of personal identity but rather you begin to better understand yourself in a much more extraordinary way. You don't need to have any type of personality to accomplish something like this; nothing is required of you other than to practice simple thought and emotional changes. You will not only create peace and joy within yourself but you will consciously tap into the ride that you are here to take. I've experienced several levels of shifting and the shift just happens as a result of the changes I decide to make. It's very important for you not to pressure yourself with goals and expectations, not to get discouraged but to just practice, you will see and feel the shift for yourself.

I was laying in bed over a year ago, full of anxiety and stress, thinking "I can't live like this anymore". I felt like I was on the verge of a breakdown. I feared that I might lose my sanity and this was pretty much my first step, my first understanding that **I** was doing something wrong. Throughout my life, my intentions were to live an extraordinary life, but from the way life seemed to be flowing, I was going about it the wrong way. That intention is still with me but instead I'm taking a different path.

I constantly tried to control everything in my life. I thought by having control I could ensure success. I wanted full influence of where my life was going. I would force things to be or for things to happen a certain way in order to keep it all on track. I needed to make sure my life was lived exactly the way I wanted it to be lived and whoever wanted to be involved, needed to follow suit; whatever hardships and stress I felt, I assumed was just part of the process.

I became aggravated and stressed with trying to keep up with what everyone should be doing; all the "corrections" I felt like I needed to make and all these responsibilities I had was just making me feel wired. More friction and bullshit were happening in my life and I felt like I was just barely keeping myself sane. My kids were stressing me out, my relationship was stressing me out, I could barely get a grip on my finances and the more anxious and upset I felt inside the more disruption developed on the outside.

It was in this stage of absolute disgust and frustration with how I felt that I realized that if everyone and everything else isn't happening the way I want it to happen then I must be trying to control the wrong things. It wasn't everything else that needed to change, it was **me**. Instead of frantically working on what others should be doing and how things should be, I realized that the only true control I have over anything here is myself. **I** am the one who feels all tangled up inside, **I** am the one who has the problems, and it was quite freeing to raise my arms and say "fuck what everyone else is doing". Just by how I felt in that moment, I knew immediately that I figured something out. That feeling of relief and excitement, I know now, was my inner being harmonizing.

INCEPTION

I was getting in my own way. Intellectually knowing this is one thing, but implementing and changing my behaviour is where the real transformation came in. I researched those who have some kind of realization and began reading and listening to teachings from different philosophers and spiritual teachers such as Eckart Tolle, Deepak Chopra, Sadhguru, Allan Watts, just to name a few. They all have similar philosophies but different teachings and they all have helped open my mind to this whole experience. There is so much information to take in that I still continue to go back to their teachings. Their common notion is that life is happening right now and that we can be joyfully and fully immersed in this very moment. I first read a book written by Abraham Hicks, and if you have ever read or heard of Abraham Hicks then you know a lot of their teachings focus on the law of attraction. It was an awesome, inspirational read but I wasn't ready at that moment to fully understand that concept, I needed to shift before I could truly understand. But what I did understand at that time was that I emit a certain vibration of energy and the vibrations I am sending out pretty much maps out my life. Everything on the planet is vibrational, research it, it's actually quite fascinating to learn. The feeling you have in your heart when you feel joy, the feeling you have in your stomach when you feel anger, are emotions that vibrate at certain frequencies. If you feel a certain way for a long period of time, and if you take notice, you'll see that what's happening around you seems to reflect those emotions. What's incredible, is how easy it is to adjust your vibe when you notice that you are emitting negative energy.

Here's a few scenarios:

1. You wake up late in the morning and are rushing around frustrated trying to get yourself and whoever else out the door. That energy jolt of frustration is being emitted into your environment. With that start to your day, you may notice you are hitting more red lights than usual, or you happen to get stuck behind a very slow driver on the road and the frustration just builds throughout the day. After a rushed, frustrating day you end up back home and just a comment from someone about why dinner hasn't started yet, a comment that would normally cause some annoyance, ends up causing you to lose your shit and the vibe keeps rolling on from there until you go to bed upset hoping for a better day.

2. Same morning, but instead this time you wake up early, you sit down quietly in your cozy home and pump yourself up for a great day. You have the extra time to get yourself and whoever else ready and out the door and feel as though you are flowing with a particularly calm vibe. You notice there's no line in the coffee drive through, you coast through nothing but green lights and the rest of your day just feels smooth. You get home and that same comment is made to you and it not only just rolls off your shoulder but instead you react with laughter. The rest of your day goes by with you feeling light hearted and at ease, and you go to bed feeling relaxed and thankful for the wonderful day.

3. Same morning, you wake up late, and the rush is about to start. Your first instinct is to scramble your mind with thoughts on how you need to get your ass moving and then you notice the feeling of rush and frustration. You take a

moment to recognize how you feel and this time you stop it in its tracks. Instead of feeling like you have to run around and run out the door, you take 1 to 2 minutes to centre yourself with a few deep breaths and you calmly get your shit together, focus on one thing at a time and get out the door. You hit the first red light and instead of going back to that frustrating feeling, you accept what is, take a couple breaths to centre yourself and continue on. You get home after work, the same ignorant comment about dinner is made to you and you're a little annoyed but you say nothing and leave it be. You go to bed that night, proud of how you were able to get control of your vibe and aim to wake up early the next day.

The 3rd scenario truly represents the behaviour changes that you will be doing throughout your transformation. It will be a constant reminder to disconnect from your thoughts, a constant step back to control your emotions. It's not hard to do, it's actually gratifyingly challenging, you continue to level up and you will feel fully supported by life through it. I haven't experienced any kind of trauma that has made me automatically shift and I haven't spent an intense amount of time meditating so this is a more technical, step by step way of accomplishing all this; I've done this the way that works for me and my life and I feel a lot of people will be able to relate.

I WANT TO FEEL GREAT

All we want is good feelings, we want consistent, grounded happiness, and not just for ourselves but for others. But the whole purpose of me spending this past year doing this was because **I** wanted to feel centered and happy. I found more than I could have imagined and I continue to discover more. Doesn't matter at what end of the social system you live, or where you think you are in life, if you feel like shit then you don't feel connected with life, and you want to connect to life, that's where the sweet spot is. I cannot think of one good reason as to why we should be feeling on edge and all quivery inside; life is meant to flow with ease. I found a way to this heightened space by practicing what I write in this book. I am experiencing a life transformation and it is beyond what I can explain, and it is attainable for anyone who chooses. Balance, appreciation, clarity, love and joy is the essence of my life experience now.

My first course of actual action was to observe my feelings. The more I observed, the more I began to question whether it was necessary to feel the way I felt in certain situations. I began calling myself out about where those feelings were truly coming from; for every situation that caused me to feel any anxiety, or stress or anger I asked myself "what am I bothered by?". A lot of situations seemed to bother me, so it was clear that there was some kind of unbalanced flow happening within myself. There were many reasons I came up with as to why I felt the way I felt, most of the reasons were blamed on someone or something else, and my mind would try to convince me that my reasoning was valid. A lot of the same thought patterns and the same emotional cycles were happening, and it didn't take me too long to see that most of my root "problems" came out of control and fear.

I used to spend a lot of time thinking about how my partner doesn't help me out as much at home and with the kids as he should. It's clear that I have much more responsibilities them him, and I noticed that these thoughts would come up when I was having to do something that I didn't want to do or when I felt overwhelmed with a responsibility. The one thought of "why he couldn't give me a hand with the kids", would turn into a thought of how he's selfish, he's taking advantage of me, which would turn into a thought of how he's not committed to me and so on. I would go from feeling annoyed about the housework to full on angry about how I'm being taken advantage of in literally 1 minute's time. I began to feel resentful which would obviously lead into arguments.

During those moments, when my thoughts were just chirping, I always had the choice to piss myself off or not, and most of the time I chose to piss myself off. Because of the stress from my relationship, the energy I was emitting was attracting even more bullshit from other areas in my life. There was alot of thinking habits that I had to change. I understand how much easier it may have been to transform if I was alone but I built a family here and I have several people who are a part of my existence; my journey requires me to learn to morph in harmony with those involved.

> *A lot of my final revisions for this book were done during the COVID pandemic and being home with everyone had just furthered my assurance that these practices absolutely transformed me and have created a much more balanced and peaceful experience here, even if others aren't feeling that same vibe.*

I went a couple months observing my emotions and behaviours. It became quite clear that my emotions could change in a matter of seconds with just a thought, no wonder I felt so unbalanced. We are vibrational beings, everything in this universe is, and my vibe seemed to change several times throughout the day. I thought about how unbalanced my outside world seemed to be and how unbalanced my inner world felt and it became clear that they reflect each other. If I can get a steady, good vibe going within myself, my outside world should reflect that....and it did.

You are not your thoughts, and if choose to take this journey on, you will realize this soon enough. You have a choice in which thoughts you want to receive. Your emotions will tell you which thoughts you should receive and which thoughts you should neglect. If a thought is making you feel bothered or upset, you can train your brain to neglect those thoughts, either cut them off before you even complete the whole thought, or by allowing those thoughts to pass without being phased. Our brains have better shit to do then to spend energy thinking about any petty ass bullshit. We have taken the luxury of having a brain and have turned it against ourselves. Now to even go further, your thoughts also attract and brand your experiences. Your thoughts produce vibrational emotions and also form your perspective, which creates the world as you see it. Your thoughts are what can fuck shit up for you if you don't get them in check. Right now, your thoughts control YOU, once you shift, YOU will be the one to control the thoughts. For me now, there isn't a thought that can cause me to feel bothered that will last more than 10 seconds, if that. I have trained my brain to disregard any bullshit thinking by recognizing that I do have a choice in what I think and focus on.

Just like the example I used about my partner, your thoughts can take you from a simple annoyance to a full blown problem. Before you add gas to that fire, you can recognize your emotions and begin to call yourself out on why you are allowing yourself to feel like that. You can do this by asking yourself questions like, What's the actual problem? Why am I bothered? Is it even valid enough to fuck myself up about it? and, most importantly, What can I do to change my vibe **now**? At first, you're going to want to put responsibility onto someone or something else because that's what your mind has been disciplined to do, but the trick is that the right answer can never include any other pronoun but **I**.

As I sit here to write, my partner continues to talk to me even though he can clearly see that I'm engaged in this, even though just yesterday I had expressed to him that I wanted more time to focus on my writing. My thoughts begin chirping about how ignorant he's being and that he doesn't give a shit that I'm focussed on this, and I start to notice tension inside my body. I've practiced this enough now to know that I cannot ride that wave for too long or follow any thoughts that are going to piss me off. Instead, I acknowledge that I'm beginning to feel tense and just allow those thoughts to pass; I'm aware that they are just thoughts that serve no purpose. I continue to type but he starts singing loudly around me and he may well be doing it on purpose to get a reaction from me. I feel the annoyance creeping back, so this time I take a couple seconds to explain to him that I'm focussed on something right now and I continue to type. Within a minute he's back at it, he's purposely doing it and he's straight up being a bozo looking for a reaction. This is apart of my existence, I live with several other beings and I can't just leave when I feel annoyed. I give myself options as to what **I** can do in this moment. I have a choice to follow thoughts, piss myself off and possibly blow up but instead I provide myself with other options.

I can try to reason with him to back off, I can remove myself from the area, I can put my laptop down and give in, or I can try to ignore it and refocus on what I'm doing. Whatever the choice is, the one option I don't give myself anymore is to sit there annoyed and continue to think about how much he's bothering me. I ended up putting the laptop away and giving in, that for me and for what

I'm trying to accomplish, was the best choice. I am working at changing my vibes and this is all a part of that. It's not a style of just letting others walk all over me or anything like that, I'm vocal when I need to be. Instead, it's a style of taking it easy until easy just becomes. No feeding the fire, no lashing out; I am pretty much attempting to vanquish my own bothered feelings rather than magnify it.

When I used to lash out angrily at someone, the anger would often turn to guilt and the guilt would turn back into anger, and instead of taking responsibility for my emotions, I would think up very particular justifications as to why I felt upset; using every other pronoun other than **I**. By taking the time to ask myself the questions as to what I'm bothered by, I realized what the root of the issue is, my thoughts, and I began to pick away at whatever bullshit excuses I used to feel like shit.

Sometimes we feel like shit for no reason at all, and those times are a little harder to analyse. I could wake up feeling sick, or tired, or hormonal and I would start my day with low energy and feeling particularly annoyed. Annoyance is like a cringe that sticks with you, it usually brings on feelings of entitlement and before I know it, I'm getting upset with everyone because I get the feeling as though they are disturbing my inner peace. I would raise my voice a little louder, give my kids a harder time about nonsense, start shit with my partner; a "try me, I dare you" kind of vibe. I could honestly just wake up like that and my whole day would be a struggle. Instead of trying to fully change my vibe in those times, I would first accept that I felt like shit but not allow my thoughts to amplify any of it. Just that acceptance of, "ok I feel like shit today and so be it", actually made me feel better and gave me a boost of energy to work with. At any point during a day like that, it's also beneficial to take 15 minutes to go sit down somewhere alone and get yourself better centered; listen to music, do push ups, take deep breaths, whatever you can do, just give yourself enough time to make a small vibrational shift, it will change your day. This is all part of the process, and the process itself is what brings on the results of freedom.

Whatever the situation is, you need to remember that first off, you don't control what's happening in your environment, and secondly, you have a choice as to what influence your thoughts are going to have on your emotions and actions. The bulk of these practices revolve around changing and clearing out thought. I never felt like I was bottling up my thoughts and emotions through this, I just became more aware that a lot of it is nonsense and when you recognize that kind of nonsense you can't be bothered to waste your energy on it.

LIFE HAPPENS

We have no control over life, we can't control what happens outside of ourselves (at least not the way we try to), and when you try to grip it into order, all you do is suffocate yourself and everyone around you. When you try to force things to be, you know just by the feeling of stress and anxiety, that you're wrong. Through all these adjustments I have been able to open myself up and things just become obvious when you get to that space. These simple practices I write about are just ways at opening yourself up, the shift itself is something that happens on its own. And when you shift, you realize, among many other things, that life is always just happening and you, just as well, are happening to life. There's nothing to clench to, everything is morphing and you are morphing with it all. Isn't that such a relief? You can say fuck it! You cannot be in control, you cannot control another being, and you cannot force anything without it boomeranging back and hitting you right in the ass. If we're going with life, (which, either way, we always are), we might as well be easy and joyful about it.

Being a mother is one of the proudest purposes I choose to have in life. I started early at 16 years old and I now have 3 girls ages 20, 13 and 4, and a 9 year old step son; it's challenging being an engaged parent. I don't believe that anyone knows the "right way" to raise little people, some much less than others, but neverless we are all in the dark for the most part. My parenting is far from traditional and has changed even farther from tradition throughout this. My view of life and our education system has changed, and it's a bit challenging to incorporate my realizations into my parenting because I still feel responsible for them while they are young. I spend a lot of my energy on them, and there's discipline, housework and meals, they do things that affect me, and it's a very personal relationship that I am still trying to balance with. I had to stop trying to correct their behaviors, I had to stop trying to push my own beliefs and ideas on them because I'm practicing non-control.

Regardless of how much I try to influence them, they will take their own paths and by rights, they should. They are experiencing life in their own reality and I don't tell them anymore how they should be living. If anything, I've observed them so much differently lately, and their connections to their own inner beings inspires and teaches me. I have to go with life in order to get past me trying to force it and that includes kids, partners, whoever and whatever happens around me. All I want for my children is happiness; the only thing that makes sense for me as a parent is that if I am at my best then that's the greatest influence I can have.

I have a partner and I knew that my relationship was going to be the biggest challenge for me when it came to this journey; my partner has at times seemed like a nemesis during this. He affects my life more than anybody, we spend most of our time together, he upsets me more than anybody, he challenges me, he did not understand me and there was a lot I needed to work through so that my relationship didn't get in the way of my shift. We have different points of views and we still have arguments, nothing close to like we used to have but it occasionally still happens. Moving away from stressful emotion and nonsense thinking is hard when you live with someone who makes you feel and think all kinds of stuff. My relationship also takes much credit for my realization, it has challenged me in remarkable ways and I have broken through many layers with the behavioural changes I have made towards my relationship.

I started observing our habits during arguments, and these arguments would be like a whole day if not a couple days, which isn't necessary. Ok to argue, shit happens, but if you're trying to get anywhere through this, arguments need to come and go quickly. I realized that I would rethink my argument points and rehearse those points through my mind and then try to go back to have them heard. This was a constant cycle; I would never get anything across and more arguments would start. The more I needed to get my point across, the worse things got. I needed to stop trying to get my side voiced in order to allow the argument to come and go. When I would catch myself feeling angrier and thinking about what was said and what I should do, I'd pull out the options card. Am I going to piss myself off and go for another round of back and forth, or am I trying to better my life? Doesn't matter what happened or what was said, if I'm not gonna quit my relationship over it then I want to move on with my day. I realize that I can't expect to have others conform to my changes, which means that anything that needs to be sorted out in my outer world, needs to be done within myself first. Instead of trying to "talk things out", I'll just use that energy to work at changing my thoughts and my own vibe.

When you are thinking something that you know is not going to add to your journey to peace, you need to remind yourself that you don't have to think about it. If you choose to think about it, you'll probably feel worse. Are you searching for peace and happiness? Of course, you're gonna answer yes, so then make that immediate choice to change your focus when you come across these situations. That's really the big "trick" to getting past shitty emotions and shitty thoughts. CHANGE WHAT YOU ARE FOCUSSING ON! Doesn't need to be something positive about the situation or positive about anything, it's harder to get to a happy thought when you are upset, but you can think about anything neutral, or start making a grocery list...whatever, think of a banana if you have to, just get your focus off the bullshit for long enough that you feel your vibe has changed.

In my relationship now, if arguments arise with my partner, I don't say much at all, and not because I hold it in but because I genuinely don't care to waste my time on it anymore. That's a perk when you shift, you hold no resentment, no anger, you just don't bother. I still get upset in that moment, I sometimes tell him he's being a dick or give him the middle finger but now instead of dragging it on, trying to be right and feeling bothered, I am actually able to walk away and change my mood immediately and not give a shit; we are both better off that way. I do whatever I can to change my focus and then I let it go; these are great moments for anyone to practice awareness. It's as simple as this: Does any action need to be taken at that moment? If so, do it, if not then move on with your day. Yep, you might be all wired up and pissed off, but that's when you go to practice your vibe change and do whatever you can to upgrade yourself into a better feeling zone. You're not always going to need to walk away and center yourself during moments of intense emotion, it gets easier and will eventually feel so natural once you have broken through your old habits.

Our relationship has changed dramatically since my perception has changed, and even though he hasn't shifted, there is now peace where there used to be conflict. There's a deeper understand of what our relationship actually is. The "changes" I wanted from myself, him and our relationship are manifesting, and it's magical to experience. I have accepted that my partner, my kids, and everyone in this world are on their own journeys and that I can't control any of their lives just like they can't control mine. The pressure of perfecting my surroundings is gone because I have realized that everything is perfect as is. I am on a journey to some kind of conscious realization whilst living with others who aren't, and I don't need to avoid my family to be at peace, they are a part of me and are coming with me. I need to give them space to live and to give myself space to be. There's no doubt that these people will continue to challenge me, but instead of allowing those moments to take away my chill, I do what I can to change my focus. My go to's are music, basketball, art, cleaning, writing,

SNL, Family Guy, Seinfeld....whatever I can do to change my vibe. As simple as it is, it's a no brainer for me, feel like shit or not? I did this every time I felt upset and now, I barely get upset at all in the first place. I no longer feel the need to be right; even if my point is right, I don't feel the need to drill that in anyone's head. It doesn't matter who's right, none of that shit matters in my life anymore.

Things can be felt in the moment but then leave it at that; the moment is the moment and when it's gone it should also be gone from you. Trust that your life is worth much more than you feeling like shit over pettiness and you'll begin to unburden yourself from the pressure. Observe your emotions and the thoughts that are attached to them, ask yourself those deep questions, call yourself out on petty bullshit and get real about why you feel what you feel. Observe the antagonizing thoughts that always seem to creep in and take time to file through them and to get rid of them. Little by little you will become a master at not wasting time thinking about shit that doesn't align with where you are trying to be. Life is happening to you just as much as you are happening to life; you can't control what happens but you can control how you happen and if you take the time to realize that most of your thoughts are nonsense, then you are on your way to changing your perception.

OVERTHINKING

I never considered the fact that I would overthink; I believed I would just think what I thought and that's what life was. A lot of these thoughts have been a waste of my life, some made me feel insecure, weak, paranoid, anxious and scared. I didn't know how to disconnect from my thoughts because I didn't know it was even an option; I thought that's who I was.

I began to question my thoughts, they didn't make me feel good and that couldn't be right. I began reading about our thoughts and thought patterns, and I started to distrust my mind. We don't remember everything as it happened in its realest form. Think about any memory of a moment you've experienced. Try to pick a memory that you don't have a picture of. How do you see yourself in that memory? From my own research and experience, our memories are visualized as tho you are watching yourself on a screen. Not seeing the memory as tho you are experiencing it all over again through your own eyes, but rather as tho you are pretty much hovering around the whole experience. Why is that? I don't know, but that right there tells me that I've never been sure of something. We don't hear every word being spoken in its truest form. Words can get narly depending on moods and openness to receive them, and the same goes for all our life experiences. We normally focus on what our mind chooses to focus on and completely block out everything else. Filters such as biases and opinions play a huge role in what our minds decide to focus on and we really fill in the rest with imagination. We think about what has happened or what we're about to do more than anything else, we just think way too damn much and it's not healthy. I am not experienced enough to explain how our brains work but if you do your own research on this you'll better understand your own thought process.

When you begin your own observation you also begin to feel like you're separating from something that many people refer to as the ego, and at the beginning, I did feel the separation. But now I realize my ego is still here but it has now joined with my inner being; as tho they are on the same page now. It started with realizing how much my thoughts were wasteful and it started with no longer carrying any guilt when negative thoughts arised, and instead of judging myself for them, I began to recognize them as silly thoughts that are irrelevant to who I truly am. Realizing this didn't immediately change or fully stop the momentum of the thought cycles, but it did give me a platform to work on; thoughts, emotions, vibes were my main 3 focuses during this shift. I just kept observing and changing.

GURU

There's many philosophers out there with different insights and different ways of explaining their enlightenment and the power of being aware. These philosophers speak from a much different life experience than myself, and when I used to listen to them speak, they it sounded so simple, to just be in the present moment. They have this confidence and peacefulness to them that is so intriguing and inspiring that I indulged in their teachings. I was so excited about what I was learning and I naively jumped into this "I am Zen" feeling as if I had it all figured out. My expectations for inner change were much more ambitious than I realized and that's pretty much why I decided to break it down through my own practices.

I spent a lot of time trying to force my mind to think positive and loving thoughts. At first, I would just try to stop my thoughts, even tell myself to shut up, but they wouldn't stop and I felt more like I was suppressing my thoughts and causing more stress than anything. I began meditating a few times a week but still not much was changing for me. As time and my practices went on, I began feeling more agitated with myself for not reaching the level of peace that I felt like I should be at; I'd take 1 step forward and then 2 steps back. I was aiming to be more like a guru when I can't even get through the day without overthinking or thinking something negative. If someone pissed me off and I thought "what an asshole" I would feel guilty for even thinking such a thing, even though that person was an asshole. I can't always feel love and patience, I can't always see the best in everyone or in myself. I was trying to force myself to be zen, and because of that I was stuck.

So what did I do? I stopped trying to be somekind guru and decided to go with my own flow. I became eager to discover more about myself and life. I used this wonderful brain to figure this out and began reading science and philosophy. I became full of wonder and questions that seem to be never ending. For every question that I answer, more questions come, this has helped change a lot for me and has opened my mind to how truly trippy life is. All this information has helped me piece together my own philosophy to life which has given me a strong platform to center on.

MY PHILOSOPHY

Life is weird and phenomenal; this planet, the creatures, nature, humans...this world is beautifully complex and yet in perfect harmony all at the same time. We've gotten so used to our surroundings that we have forgotten how fascinating life really is. We are here for an unknown purpose, not just unknown to me but unknown to every single living creature on this planet. We can hypothesise all we want but when it comes down to it, we don't know shit. I went through all possible purposes to my life such as religion, family, money and I came to the determination that I'm here to just experience life and I am just as much a part of this world as this world is a part of me.

We feel as though we are always searching for something and usually fill that void with all kinds of different things such as relationships, kids, work, intoxicants, money, sex, exercise, food, philanthropy, - we search for anything that brings us some type of meaningfulness and joy until we lose that feeling and look for more. Nothing wrong with taking part in any of these but we seem to attach our happiness to it and once life changes (cause it always does) we're all fucked up about it. I've attached myself to every single one of those void fillers and know first hand that what I was searching for I've had all along.

All we are searching for is happiness; that's the bottom line search. Oh, but you wanna save the world? Nope, you wanna feel as though you saved the world. Oh, but you wanna be the best artist, athlete, writer or whatever? Nope, you wanna feel as though you are the best.....I could do this all day. Bottom line- you wanna feel good and you assume that that kind of constant happiness will only come after you've accomplished whatever goal you've set for yourself. Well, I'm sure by now you've already accomplished many goals- are you consistently happy yet? Are you finally able to sit back and enjoy life to its fullest? That peace and happiness doesn't come at a later date, it's something available right now and is always available now; this is why I chose to focus on myself.

We don't often feel as though we have the time for self care, and I needed time to work at quieting my mind and to work at re-inventing my perspective of life. I don't have hours a day to sit quietly and observe, I have responsibilities in my life that take up alot of my time and energy. I had to come up with ways to craft this into my world. Complete peace doesn't need to be your goal, if it is it may take you several lifetimes to achieve, but being happy, free and centered is attainable and because of these small life changes that I made, I can confidently say that I have never been happier. I feel free and secure, I'm experiencing manifested desires in all areas of my life. If I can do this, so can YOU.
Create your own philosophy, the search itself is life changing even if you don't come up with one.

ENGAGE WITH LIFE

How connected do you feel with life? Are you conscious most of the time or are you too preoccupied to notice? I feel as though I was in some kind of robotic trance prior to this shift; day in, day out same shit, my mind occupied with all kinds of insignificant bullshit that had nothing to do with the present moment. I was spending most of my life living inside my own head rather than being conscious. We use up time just thinking of what needs to be done next or what happened earlier; life is too amazing to be living that way and it's not a requirement of being human.

There's a difference between being alive and actually experiencing life. When I began to observe my thoughts I quickly realized that most of my day was spent in compulsive, useless thought. I thought through my entire day; narrating or thinking about something that had nothing to do with where I was or what I was doing at the moment. That's too much thinking for nothing. I'm trying to work at being in the present moment so I started picking away at the nonsense thinking. I began taking tabs on the times that my mind was most active with insignificant thoughts such as what time I'll be doing laundry at or what happened earlier at work. I caught myself in many moments completely lost in my mind, and interestingly I realized I spent a lot of time thinking about what I'm about to do next. I don't need to keep reminding myself about what I'm gonna do next.

When you get into this practice you'll notice your own types of thought cycles and you'll want to come up with different ways of breaking those cycles. Many of my mornings start with kid prep for school, send them off, drive the same drive to work, work at the same job I've had for over 10 years, drive the same drive back and so on. I do this day in and day out, sometimes without even being conscious of the whole day. It was repetitive and boring; same shit, so instead of being focussed in the actual moment I would think nonsense while robotically tending to my "life chores". Routines bore our minds, and our minds have a habit of filling in that boredom with all kinds of unnecessary thoughts. This is the norm I think for most people, which in turn unfortunately, makes it the norm to be completely out of touch with life. All these moments that we spend mindlessly thinking about nonsense can be used to start practicing how to shift.

The idea is to be engaged in life, there's this constant vibrational exchange happening between you and the world you exist in, and if you want the best results with life you must be aware of this exchange as much as possible. You want to be involved with life while it is happening in that moment. When you find yourself caught up in that robotic manner, wake yourself up by slowing down and refocusing on what you are doing. Focus is the key that helps quiet down the mind and places you in the moment. Car rides, showering, dishes, work; these are all situations where my thoughts would just run. Depending on the moment, I'll do a few things, I will either listen to some good music, or I will practice focussing on what I'm doing in that moment. Sometimes just closing my eyes for a few seconds helps reset my mind. Whatever you can do to break the cycle of compulsive thinking. It's just a matter of training your brain to a new process of how you will do things.

I often have headphones on my ears. Music is such a powerful tool for me in this. I listen to every genre of music, it has the ability to keep me in the moment and lift my good energy. I have a playlist of songs that give me all kinds of good feelings. To help me get past any anger or sadness I can go through my playlist and when that one song comes on that my body just reacts to immediately,

I allow myself to be fully engaged in the music and my energy changes. Movement is another powerful tool for me, basketball is my go to, I'm fully engaged in that moment and it just lifts my vibes.

There are plenty of moments during the day to work at clearing out your mind of bullshit, compulsive thinking, and to remind yourself to be engaged in life. All this goes hand in hand with calming your emotions and allowing yourself to open up to the space you are in. It's training, it's not rigorous, there's no rush to all this and no pressure. You have plenty of moments to practice and you will witness the changes from the beginning.

WHAT'S THE REAL PROBLEM?

You've lived long enough to know that things are always changing, and that when times have been tough you've gotten through. So why do you still spend precious time worrying? People believe that worry and stress comes from having responsibilities and creates progress, but the truth is worrying does absolutely nothing positive for you. In fact, worrying creates anxiety and I believe that anyone reading this book is sick as fuck over feeling anxiety and stress. I've noticed there's two sides to this, my mind could bring on the thoughts of worry but my body can also activate those thoughts with just an uneasy feeling in my stomach. Be aware that this can go both ways and ask yourself in those moments if there's anything right now that is actually happening to cause that feeling. Chances are nothing is actually happening, otherwise you'd be in action instead of in thought; worry is nothing but thought and it's not beneficial or productive. I know that you're thinking, yeah, yeah, everyone knows that worrying isn't beneficial, but I'm also throwing "concern", "caring about certain things and how they should be" into this category...it's the same damn thing just on a different scale. Either aren't beneficial, if you hold onto either, then you aren't ready to shift. You have to have faith and believe that life is supporting you. If anything narly is going on or going to happen in your life, chances are you brought it on with worry, concern and control issues.

We spend time worrying about worst case scenarios of what might happen; health, finances, family. Life is uncertain and anything can happen but worrying doesn't prepare you for that, most likely the worrying will just attract it. Think about your biggest fear that causes you to worry, now face it. Go through every possible scenario as though it's actually happening to you and face it all. You will see that in the end there really is nothing to fear because death is always inevitable and when you die, shows over and nothing you did or didn't do even matters.

We spend time worrying about all the things we need to get done. I understand what it's like to live with multiple responsibilities; I used to spend a lot of time thinking about all the shit I need to do and then more thoughts would pop up adding more shit. I decided at the beginning of my transformation that I get to pick what matters to me and my priorities will reflect that. When my mind would be concerned about something that might need to get done, I first asked myself, "am I going to do this right now?" If yes, then ok, get it done. If the answer is no then I'm not gonna give a shit right now, I'm too busy in whatever I'm doing at that moment. I have a to do list and whenever I think about something that needs to be done, I write it on my list. That list serves two great purposes for me: 1. By writing it down, I release it from my mind. 2. I actually get more shit done with that list, whenever I get the feeling of boredom I look at the list and complete something off it. I better organize myself to better set myself up, I stopped doing things for others that I didn't want to do. I stopped offering others help unless it's needed in the moment, I stopped saying yes all the time and pre-planning all kinds of things; I just stopped putting pressure on myself about anything.

We worry about what other people think and how they feel; we will disrupt our own life for others. If you want to live in your truth you need to understand that your choices and behaviour cannot be influenced by others and by what others might think. What if when you die, you find out that this whole time, it's just been you and everyone else are just bots, lets say for fun. All those times you wanted to ride your grocery cart down the parking lot or all those dreams you wanted to chase but you cared too much what other's might think. Think about it, you are in your own individual human body, experiencing life through your own perception; including other people's judgements only gets in the way of your freedom to live.

If I worry about how my actions may affect somebody else then I'm just feeding unconscious bullshit anyways. I'm not out to hurt anyone and I am confident that my actions should not affect anyone in a negative way, and if they feel offended for whatever I do or don't do, then that's their own issue to deal with. I stopped trying to rearrange my world in order to make others feel comfortable. I'm going with my flow, not looking to interfere in anyone else's flow, and not going to change my pace because of someone else's unconscious thoughts.

You will live through good and bad times, that's inevitable because life is full of it all. You should expect the unexpected because the only guarantee we have in life is death. Nobody knows where we go after this, there's a lot of speculation but not one single living creature here knows. This helps me not to take life too seriously and to appreciate the fact that I'm in this crazy world. We could come up with a neverending list of things to concern ourselves with, it does not save you from anything, it's not "responsible" to worry, and you have a choice. If you got time to sit down and worry about things then you got time to challenge those thoughts and to practice being aware.

LET IT ALL GO

The reality is that the past and future are only present in your imagination. You are either aware in the moment or you are imagining a past or future moment. Don't try and argue with that point because you can't. There's nothing that you need to dig up from your past to try to overcome or to learn a lesson from; everything is now. If you are still thinking about shit that happened in the past and are on this journey to shift you are going to be floored with how easy letting go will be. I used to blame others when I felt like shit, I would act in anger and in resentment towards others that I felt had hurt me. One of the biggest transformations for me was that I could only look to myself if I felt any kind of emotion. Doesn't matter what other people do or say, if I felt a certain way then I needed to take responsibility for that feeling. Knowing this changed my whole perspective of people and situations that I would have deemed as unfair, which helps me not to judge others for their own actions also.

Quite a few years ago my partner had cheated on me, I am no innocent victim but at the time I sure felt like one. I've been on both sides of infidelity in my life, so I'm all around aware of the chaos that it turns into and trust becomes a major issue that puts a lot of fear on both sides. I played the immediate victim and stayed in that role for a very long time. My mind continued to tell me that I was a victim, which gave me that privilege to pretty much act whichever way I wanted and to always hold that "you owe me" status. This went on for months and made our environment really shitty and I never once during those months thought that maybe I was the one who created the whole situation. It wasn't time that healed it, it wasn't that he had "fixed" the situation, it was the choice that I made to let it go. I first looked at the role I played in all this, and the choices that brought me to this point, and I took full responsibility for the life I live. After accepting the situation, I let that shit go, we both let it go. If I was choosing to continue my life with him and if I am rooting for us as a family then I have to give it my best. If my journey is for peace, love and joy then I had no choice but to let it go. I stopped bringing it up, I worked at changing each thought that brought me back and within months I stopped thinking about it. I don't fear the thoughts, I just don't have the desire to waste my time on them anymore.

Whatever pain you have felt or any pain that you are feeling now, you gotta let that shit go. That means stop having whatever pity party you are having for yourself, that means stop thinking about it and stop **talking** about it. Now is all that matters, now is the only reality happening. If the same problem keeps coming up and a cycle evolves, sometimes changing your environment is the only way to let that shit go.

Anytime you get stuck on something that is bothering you and you can't seem to figure out how to work through it, remind yourself that the only moment that matters is now, focus on being engaged in the moment and revisit the subject at a better time. This works because basically you can keep sloughing off the issue until it gets less and less bothersome and if a choice needs to be made you'll be much more centered about it. Right now do you choose to live the moment you are blessed to have or do you choose to think about hurtful and angry things? You always have that choice. Get yourself centered and cleared up and you life will reflect that.

SPEAK LESS

Since I was little, I've always talked a lot. I always had strong opinions and I was pretty vocal about my stances. We seem to want to share our "life lessons" or give people advice but most people don't take unsolicited advice too well, it feels condescending and instead of getting a point across you've actually made it more difficult for them to receive it. I learned to speak less not just for others but for myself. If you notice, most people talk just to hear themselves and I did the same; I'll speak my mind if asked but other than that I've gotten pretty quiet about opinions, mostly because I no longer carry much opinions. I can only speak to my own existence, that's all I truly know. As you shift, you begin to realize how powerful words are if you are attaching emotions to them. Speaking falls into the same category as thinking when it comes to how it reflects into your world. It also becomes inevitable to speak less during this because your thoughts will be less prevalent and your flow and actions will do most of the communicating.

When I had been in a heated exchange with someone, my mouth would just run cause my mind was fired up. During the beginning of this process, I knew that it would be hard to stop my mind from thinking during conflicted situations, especially when my body continues to remind me with that anxious feeling in my stomach. Instead of trying to fight my thoughts off I started with just keeping my mouth shut. I acknowledged that my thoughts would be amped and upsetting but the first stage of being able to clear those thoughts is not to control them but to not make anything worse with words. This should always be in the back of your mind when you take this journey on, speak less.

If you feel like shit you shouldn't be talking. Once you master that, you can begin working on not allowing those thoughts to piss you off. I've spent a lot of time thinking that I know what's right and that if only my partner and my kids could see through my eyes then everything will be perfect. I realized that it doesn't matter how much I think I know or how much I believe what path is right, they are their own being, they see life in their own perspective and I have no right to tell another person how to live. I struggled a lot with this with my family because their actions seem to condition my life. With the clarity I had begun gaining I needed to stay true to this concept more than ever because I went through a stage where all I wanted to do was talk about this transformation and try to get others to try for themselves. Writing this book has given me the opportunity to express all this. I tried to convert my partner, my kids, my friends but trying to give them information without the openness to receive it just made me feel frustrated. I no longer say much about any of this but instead just lead and I see them following at their own pace.

YOU CAN'T FIX ANYONE ELSE'S LIFE

I love helping others, I don't spend my time looking to be a helper but if I'm present in a situation when I know I can help, I will. I received a lot of support during my life and I am so grateful for it. But trying to help others can sometimes consume our own life and also cause friction in it. There may be people in your life that go through these dramatic cycles and come to you for help or advice but never actually change. You sometimes avoid them because they just make you feel anxious and that may be difficult to balance while you're in the process of this shift. If you get too involved in what's happening in their world, it will begin to affect your world. You have no business in other people's business, even when they try to make it your business.

It's fine to set boundaries with others, to tell them that you are in the process of self care and that if they need any actual help with something to let you know. Those who are truly needing your help won't feel like a burden to you. Most people, just like yourself, will need to go within themselves to change their own lives, no help from you will do it. It does nothing for their own journey to have you sit there and humour their unconciousness. Set your boundaries for your own peace and lead by example if you truly want to help.

A good example would be my daughter who struggled with drug

abuse and anxiety. It broke my heart to see her go down the path she did. I knew what she needed but I did not know how to make her realize it. I tried getting her in different therapies, I had been to the courts, hospitals etc.; doing everything I possibly could to get her out of the places she was in and to hopefully wake her up. I extended all resources that I possibly could but she just wasn't wanting the change. She would message and call me non-stop, abusive in her words at times, paranoid, hysterical and because I was so caught up with having to fix my child, I allowed all the stress, the sleepless nights and the worry. She blamed me for the situations she was in and it turned into just a chaotic, unfortunate cycle. It wasn't until I stopped trying to fix her that she began to help herself. I had to stop answering her messages and calls and I did it for my own sanity; the whole situation was so toxic that I needed to remove myself from it. This wasn't good for either of us and the only way I could stop it was by not engaging with it. I made it clear that at any point when she was ready to help herself that I would be here but her choices weren't my life and I could no longer allow her to bring me into it. She took her own path and is figuring things out for herself. I no longer try to guide her the way I think she should go and she no longer burdens me with her issues. I help her with as much as she needs, without any pressure, and we have a great relationship because of it. I don't worry about her, I know she will find her center and she's evolving at her own pace. Since I've shifted, she is now in College, has an awesome job and owns her very first car; another manifestation.

I can still feel well and happy even when those around me don't. I do feel empathy and compassion for those who are struggling, but I know the power they have within themselves and it's up to them to take that on; I don't attach myself to their own journey, I'm on my own. I feel like if I connect to their struggle I will begin to feel as though I'm struggling myself, and if you continue to help someone who creates the same problem for themselves then again you're just adding to their unconsciousness. I'm doing this for me and I can tell you after going through this shift, I am not only benefiting but everyone else around me is too. Life became peaceful without changing anything other than myself.

CONNECTIONS WILL CHANGE

Life has all kinds of characters around and you may feel a good vibe with some and others you may feel repelled by. Be cautious with who you allow close during your shift, their vibes may find its way into your own life. You don't have to keep everyone in your life, those who serve up negative vibes don't need to be close to you. This is why I've only kept those close to me who serve my life positively and those who pose more of a negative feel I keep at arms length or don't have them around at all. Yes I'm supposed to be understanding of their ignorance but at the same time I'm not equipped to take on others' baggage and I'm still learning how to find my own peace. You don't need to identify with everybody, nor does everybody need to identify with you. It's ok if you stop being around people who just aren't aligned with your views; they will move on to somebody else, they are living in their own world.

I know there are some people you can't just cut out such as parents, neighbours and even your own kids and for those instances, what I found is to not emotionally connect to their unconsciousness. During this shift, I used to try and convert these people in hopes that their perspectives would change but I learned quickly that I can't fix anybody. Regardless of how I respond to them it won't change in that way, so I figured I'd just try to not respond. I first stopped countering their talk, becoming more silent but engaged. I would have to remind myself that they have no clue just like the rest of us and that this is just a moment in my life, and just like all moments it will come and go. If a question is asked to me, my responses need to always stay aligned with myself. So depending on the situation I may be as blunt to just say, "well don't think about it". I have no desire to get involved in any unconscious bullshit and I do not want to feed it either.

If you know yourself and live in your truth then you can continue to have these people around without the effects. No need to curse these people out in your head, or even hide from them, well actually you may want to hide from them until you are better grounded but once you shift you can be around anyone without walking off your path or feeling disconnected. If you are working towards being a more enlightened being why would you ever pretend to be anyone other than yourself, you don't need to connect to everyone, and if you walked around listening to what everyone else was thinking....you wouldn't want to connect to everyone. Once you shift, those uncomfortable social situations don't feel present anymore; you shift and the world around you shifts.

FEED YOUR MIND
INSPIRATION

If you spend a lot of time watching tv or scrolling through social media, you're gonna want to change that. I encourage you to stay off social media and stay disconnected from anything that may influence you during your shift. I used to be an avid news watcher, my television often had CNN and other news media playing on it and I would get consumed with all the drama. One of the easiest, beneficial changes I made was to stop watching the news and to stay off social media. I'm not trying to ignore life because life is what is happening within me at this very moment. I don't feel the need to be aware of all the drama, pain and suffering that most news outlets magnify, apparently 90 percent of the news is negative. If I really want to inform myself on pain and suffering there's plenty around for me to notice. Just as well, if I want to inform myself on happiness and love there's also plenty around for me to notice. I choose to feed my mind now with more positive and factual information. If I feel the desire to catch up on the news, I will either scroll through a news feed, maybe read a few headlines and if something catches my attention I'll read the article or even better, I wait until the late night shows come on and get my news from people like Trevor Noah, it brings a more comical feel to it. I don't feel the need to connect to anything that isn't in my existence, so if I'm spending any time watching tv or reading articles, it's for entertainment or personal education, not to connect with. We have so much material right at our fingertips that instead of spending your time reading through facebook and all these other sites, look for inspiration and passion.

Once you get into these practices you are going to notice a sense of quietness in your mind, I don't want to call it boredom but similar to that feeling. You will have vanquished a lot of your old thought cycles and what's even more awesome than that is that you have an opportunity to fill in that extra space and time with new, good feeling information. I began looking up scientific facts on our planet and our bodies, I began reading more about different philosophers, and I have been fascinated at the magic of it all, and the eagerness for more information hasn't stopped. I made the choice to not bother placing my attention on anything that doesn't give me inspiration and that doesn't connect with my life. It's what you choose to focus on that will inevitably shape the reality that you see. It's impossible to take in everything around us, therefore we are always choosing what information we feed ourselves.

YOUR JOURNEY, YOUR VIEW, YOUR LIFE

Nobody will ever know the feelings and thoughts you have. We all have our unique perspectives and understandings that started from the moment we think we were born here. My view and my thought processes are completely unique to me, just like I cannot get behind someone else's eyes. This may be one world, but ultimately, we live in our own very unique ones. Imagine your life as though you have virtual reality goggles on, you put on someone else's goggles and you are in a whole new world. I believe we are here to be selfish and passive, it's all about my own existence; not trying to understand someone else's and not trying to interfere either.

Much of the society that I exist around looks up to fame and fortune but the truth is that many celebrities and many wealthy people cope with high anxiety, stress and mental illness. Some of the most famous comedians have committed suicide, some of the richest artists and athletes turn to drug abuse and alcoholism. I'm not saying it's wrong to want wealth and fame but I believe it's only worth attaining if you are centered enough to gracefully revel in it. I understand that regardless of what the view is from the outside, it is the view from the inside that matters because in actual reality...that's the only view I have. I will never again wish

to have anybody else's life and realizing what I have is worth more
than anything I can think of.

GRATITUDE

Most of us were told to "be thankful for what you have" and "other people have much less", I've told my kids similar things, but that's not the way to attain gratitude. Gratitude isn't being thankful for something, gratitude is a state of being that comes from being grateful and also comes as a perk with the shift. You can't help but feel gratitude when you get the sense that everything in your existence is there just for you. And you can't help but feel gratitude when you practice appreciation and thankfulness.

Your perception is going to change if you take on these practices, and gratitude is one of the biggest shifts you will notice. When I say your perception is going to change, I mean you will realize just how amazing everything around you is and how much more connected you are to it all; everything in your environment from the tree outside, to the couch you sit on or the cup you drink out of. This shift is going to help put you in a state of gratitude and when you get into it, you will feel it everywhere.

I do mantras, meditations, and I've even spent whole days thanking everything that I had in my focus; I say thank you to that first drink of coffee in the morning, to the clothes I put on, to my car when I first get into it, to the food I eat, I'll go on an all day thankfest; this is something you can begin doing while you are in the process of abolishing the compulsive thinking, helps to keep you in the moment. Those times when you actually feel thankful for something, grasp onto that feeling and continue with everything else you can think of to add.

Once I made a big enough shift to when my thought practices were no longer needed, I began a Phase II of all this. I've turned my focus more into the gratitude practices, meditation and creating. The quietness, serenity and energy that you will have once you get to this Phase II is incredible, you can start really playing with life. The opportunity to really start living will be noticeable when you are no longer occupied with all that bullshit. Time to start getting deep, like blow your fucking mind deep.

MEDITATION

I know the cringe of being told to meditate, and I know how frustrating it can be to meditate. It's hard at first to sit quietly with the intention of calming your mind cause all it wants to do in those moments is talk. It's discouraging when you'll go 15 minutes of "meditation" but your mind didn't stop the whole time. Meditation is a type of exercise, that in my experience, gets easier and easier with each practice. Without meditation I wouldn't have the quiet mind that I have now; without meditation all these changes and ideas that I've incorporated in this book wouldn't flow the way they did. Do I need to meditate on a daily basis anymore? No, but I did for a while in order to clear out my mind and to practice stillness. Did I want to meditate on a daily basis? No! Do I now, want to meditate on a daily basis? Yes! I look forward to. Once you get into it you'll get the feeling that you have all kinds of power and energy that you didn't even know you possessed. I don't believe meditation is needed, focus is similar to meditation and we focus on things everyday. For me, meditation was beneficial.

I don't have hours to go sit somewhere quietly alone, but I do have at least 15 minutes a day to get some kind of quiet time to myself. I sometimes use guided meditations, I sometimes just sit quietly alone, AUM chants (my favorite) or recite positive mantras and affirmations. It's up to you to try different ways and to find the ones that you feel work best with you. Over time it does become enjoyable and the benefits can be extraordinary.

When I first began to meditate my mind would be loud for the first 5-7 minutes but after that I would get into a meditative type state. I just stuck to my breathing and didn't pressure myself too much about the thoughts. Great time to meditate is when you're happy and feeling extra good. Whatever thoughts that pop into your mind during meditation will be happier. I only started with maybe just 3 days a week, and it took me about 3 months to commit to my meditations. As you become more and more comfortable you will actually be excited to get that time in. Besides the many scientifically proven benefits that meditation provides, I also laugh more, I feel more relaxed, I have much more patience (or I'm just not waiting for anything anymore), and I connect deeper within myself. Meditation has helped me slow down the pace, clear out the trash from my mind and helped me quiet down. I often close my eyes throughout the day; if we are watching tv during commercials, I close my eyes and just breath. If I'm waiting for something, I'll just stand there and close my eyes. All those times when you get the urge to maybe pick up your phone to surf, take that "spare time" to just close your eyes. It's a matter of just shutting down the extra energy around you and allowing your vibe to connect, that's how I see meditation.

BELIEVE

I needed to believe that this shift was possible, and really all it took was a little belief because from early in this experience I could see for myself that my world was shifting. There will be times of doubt; at times I had felt foolish and guilty for feeling so Goddamn good and there were times during my shift when I contemplated if I was sane; I would ask myself if I was living in reality. I began to notice when I talked with others that I became insensitive with what I used to connect with, and I stopped identifying with really anything that wasn't part of my actual existence. This has changed things for sure, but it's more like a shift, and everything around you will eventually shift too, it all becomes clearer, and that's what you need to believe.

We all believe in something, religion, spiritualism, some believe that hard work brings you wealth, or some believe the newspaper horoscope maps out their life; that's fine for me, this is what I choose to believe in. I've done my fair share of hard work and suffering; I've climbed out of holes, I have pushed myself through struggle and adversity, but that's not what brought me to happiness and wholeness. There is no price to pay to acquire any of this, it is something available to each and every one of us in every single moment. Believe in your ability to make this shift and there's no doubt you will succeed, those around you will begin to conform and you will look back and realize that you've woken up.

FLOW WITH IT

There is a flow with life, it is this energy driven flow that you are connected to and that you can either go with or against. When you feel anxious, angry, or bothered, you are going against the flow of life. When your mind begins to clear and you become aware of your own energy, you will begin to shift and start flowing with life. While you shift, you will undoubtedly experience the world around you shifting and you will know without a doubt, this is the relationship you are supposed to have with life.

We pre-determine our future throughout most of our days just by reminding ourselves about what we are going to do next. I literally stopped pre-planning when I was going to clean, when I was going to cook, when I would take walks, when I would shower, when I would meditate; anything that I could overlook in any given moment, I stopped preplanning. I don't have many scheduled deadlines or meetings to follow anymore so my life may be a little easier to adapt to this practice but I do have a large family and a job. Other than having to maneuver around my kids' life, this was an easy practice that has also added tremendous benefits to my shift. I'd start with a day of not telling myself what I need to do throughout the day. Instead of reminding myself that, "in an hour I'll start cooking" or "I'll shower at 7", I just went with it and moved from one thing to another, to another, just based on where life kinda took me that day.

I'll take a day off work as a good example; I used to wake up and start thinking about what I was gonna do that day. I would plan to wash the dishes, and clean up the yard, laundry, a bike ride, just all these things I thought about during the week that I pre-planned to accomplish during the weeked. And throughout the whole day I would remind myself of what I'll be doing next, I was predetermining my whole day, shit I was predetermining my whole weekend in my mind during the week.

By pre-planning, you are wasting time thinking about shit that you are going to need to do, and you're pretty much determining your future. Where's the fun in that? I don't want to know what I'm gonna be doing all the time. When I have "flow days", I will literally go from one thing to the next without any resistance and the day is always effortless and fun. There are days when I have plans, and shit needs to be timely but I just accept that I have shit to do and I plan what I need. For everything else, which is still a lot, I don't need to preplan. I know that there's certain things that are better off executed if there's somekind of pre-planning, but really everything else, like what time you're gonna eat at, is better left at just happening when you feel it should happen. Nothing about these practices feel irresponsible to me, and as you shift you'll see my point.

CREATE

When you get to a point where you have shifted enough that you no longer need to continue with most of these practices, when you have calmed your thoughts so much that you don't have much to think about anymore, you will notice a sense of calmness. With all the extra mind space you're going to gain through this, I suggest it's time for conscious creation. You've been creating the whole time, the life you are experiencing is your creation but it's been an unconscious creation for the most part. Now you have the ability to create consciously and out of passion.

Activities you feel connected to and truly enjoy being present in, any particular undertakings that give you that extra jolt of good feeling, should be visited more often now; that's where the extra spark of life comes from. I spend more time doing the things that bring me joy such as writing, hanging out with my family, basketball, hiking, painting, reading, music..whatever my little heart has been desiring- that to me is being alive.

FINAL REFLECTION

This has been a year in the making; a year of practices, shifts and changes. To think back at where I was emotionally and vibrationally to where I am now, just blows my mind. I'm not the same person and yet I feel as though I know myself completely. This works and I believe this book is gonna help others shift; I have often gone back to my writings to put me back on track, and I know that if I can do this, many others can do it too.

We are vibrational beings living in a vibrational world. Knowledge yourself on this, understand this and be aware of your own vibration as much as you can until you shift into a naturally good feeling one. Every uncomfortable feeling you have been feeling since you can remember, has always been your inner being disagreeing with your current focus. If you just take time to listen, your inner being will guide you. Once you get past that first phase of transformation, there's no need to practice much because you'll just shift into it naturally. Give yourself the worth to journey through this fully, you will find more than you expected and it will be so obvious that you'll sometimes laugh.

There will be days you will slip and feel as though you are retracting. You may come across the same old thought patterns you assumed you abolished and it is going to throw you off. Don't allow discouragement and disappointment to hold you back, those are just bullshit thoughts, and it's those discouraging thoughts that will keep you slipping. The slips are all a part of the process and those setbacks helped me realize that I've been in the right flow and the quickest way to get back into that flow is to feel good. I'd have to take it back up 1 step at a time, usually going through my own writings to get me back on track but it was always much quicker and eventually the slips don't even happen. It's been a play in progress, pulling my attention away from the outside world and observing my inner world. It's honestly not difficult, I don't feel as though I had to sacrifice anything and the practices were satisfyingly challenging.

The further I get into all this, the deeper I connect to life. There's a natural flow you will tap into more and more as you progress; it's tough to explain, but I once heard a philosoper say something on the line of "everything's the same except you feel as tho you are 2 inches off the ground", and that's a good way of describing those experiences. I know now that those moments are what others have called awareness, enlightment, clarity. I've spent days as tho I was in a daydream, feeling as tho I'm just floating with whole process of life. Those experiences are so incredible that you'll want to grasp onto it. As soon as I began to notice what "state of mind" I was in, I would get so excited and begin to notice it so much more that I'd push myself out of it. The harder you try to hold onto it the quicker it goes away. From my own experience, it started with just moments, and as I got further in this journey those moments turned into a day or two and more frequent. I've learned not to try and grasp it, but to just be. I've also learned not to talk too much about those moments; I feel like it's sacred and I'm gonna keep it as close to my heart as possible. They do come and go and I have no clue why but I don't even try to understand it anymore; you'll experience it for yourself and realize that no description could accurately explain what those moments are like.

You have a choice as to how you wanna perceive and experience life. You can continue to follow culture and society or you can begin to live in your purpose. Whether you choose to continue as you've always been or you decide to change, life will remain the same in the sense that you're here now and then you'll be dead. There's nothing to lose here but yet there's incredible abundance of all kinds of good stuff to gain. This is how it feels to truly be alive. Going for this shift has been the best choice that I ever made and I know there's still so much more to explore.

Bon Voyage!

Christine Cecile Guillot

www.ingramcontent.com/pod-product-compliance
Lightning Source LLC
Chambersburg PA
CBHW032130050726
47590CB00008B/3031